**winning
over
worry**

Other Studies in A Mom's Ordinary Day Bible Study Series

Entering God's Presence

Finding Joy in All You Are

Gaining and Being a Friend

Growing Strong with God

Making Praise a Priority

Managing Your Time

Mothering without Guilt

Jean E. Syswerda is mother to three grown children. A former editor and associate publisher at Zondervan, she was responsible for such best-selling Bibles as the *NIV Adventure Bible,* the *NIV Teen Study Bible,* and the *NIV Women's Devotional Bible 1.* She is the general editor of the *NIV Women of Faith Study Bible* and the *NLT Prayer Bible,* as well as the coauthor of the *Read with Me Bible* and the best-selling *Women of the Bible.*

six sessions

YOU & GOD . YOU & OTHERS . YOU & YOUR KIDS

mom

a mom's ordinary day
BIBLE STUDY SERIES

winning over worry

JEAN E. SYSWERDA
general editor

written by
JEAN E. SYSWERDA

ZONDERVAN™

GRAND RAPIDS, MICHIGAN 49530 USA

ZONDERVAN™

Winning over Worry
Copyright © 2003 by Jean Syswerda

Requests for information should be addressed to:
Zondervan, *Grand Rapids, Michigan 49530*

ISBN 0-310-24719-5

All Scripture quotations, unless otherwise indicated, are taken from the *Holy Bible: New International Version®*. NIV®. Copyright © 1973, 1978, 1984 by International Bible Society. Used by permission of Zondervan. All rights reserved.

Scripture quotations marked NLT are taken from the *Holy Bible, New Living Translation,* copyright © 1996. Used by permission of Tyndale House Publishers, Inc., Wheaton, Illinois 60189. All rights reserved.

All rights reserved. No part of this publication may be reproduced, stored in a retrieval system, or transmitted in any form or by any means—electronic, mechanical, photocopy, recording, or any other—except for brief quotations in printed reviews, without the prior permission of the publisher.

Interior design by Tracey Moran

Printed in the United States of America

03 04 05 06 07 08 09 /❖ CH/ 10 9 8 7 6 5 4 3 2 1

contents

7   how to use this study guide
11   introduction
13   session 1: worry's worthlessness
21   session 2: worry's critical consequences
27   session 3: worry or concern?
37   session 4: living positively or negatively
45   session 5: worry-free living
53   session 6: a weapon against worry
61   leader's notes

how to use this study guide

Hey, Mom, are you ready?

When was the last time you did something just for you?

In the joy and junk and memories and mess that is your life as a mother, do you sometimes feel that you've lost something—something essential and important?

The Bible studies in this series will help you rediscover and, even more, enjoy all the parts and pieces that make you a unique person, a unique mother, and a unique and holy creation of God.

The five sections of each individual session are designed to meet a particular need in your life—the need for time alone, for time with God's Word, for time with others, for time with God, and for time with your children. How you approach and use each section is up to you and your individual styles and desires. But here are a few suggestions:

For You Alone

The operative word here is, of course, *alone.* For moms who rarely even go to the bathroom alone, being alone can seem an almost impossible goal. Perhaps thinking in terms of *quiet* would help. You can do this part of the study in any quiet moments in your home—when kids are sleeping, when they're watching a video, when you're nursing a little one. Any quiet or personal time you can find in your own schedule will work. This part of the study is sometimes serious, sometimes fun, sometimes downright silly. It will prepare your mind for the other sections of the study.

For You and God's Word

Put this study guide, a pen, and your Bible in a favorite place— somewhere you can grab it at any free moment, perhaps in the kitchen or by a favorite chair. Then, when a few spare moments arise, everything you need is right at hand. Each of the six sessions includes a short Bible study for you to complete alone. (This doesn't necessarily mean you have to *be* alone to complete it! My daughter reads her Bible out loud during a morning bath while her infant son sits in his bouncy seat next to her. She gets her Bible read, and he's content with the sound of his mommy's voice.)

For You and Others

The third section of each study is intended for small groups (even just two is a small group!), but if that isn't possible, you *can* complete it alone. Or connect with a friend or neighbor to work through the materials together. If you function as the leader, little preparation is required; you can learn right along with your fellow mothers. The leader is actually more of a facilitator, keeping the discussion on track and your time together moving along. Leadership information on many of the questions in the "For You and Others" section is included at the back of this book, beginning on page 61.

For You and God

The fourth section of each session will guide you in a time of prayer based on the study's topic. Wonder when you'll find time to do this? Prop this book up in your window while doing dishes. God hears the prayers of moms whose hands are in dishwater! Or take it along in the car when picking up a child from an activity. Or use it while nursing an infant. These times of talking to God are precious moments in the life of a mom. And with all the demands on your time, you need to grab these moments whenever you can. Do also try, though, to find a time each day for quiet, concentrated prayer. Your children need their mom to be "prayed up" when she faces each day.

For You and Your Kids

How great is this? A Bible study that includes something for your kids as well as for you! The final section of each session gives suggestions on applying the principles of the study in your kids' lives as well as in your own. The activities are appropriately geared to different ages and range from simple to more complex.

One Important Final Note

Don't presume you have to move through these sessions in any particular order. The order in which they appear in each study is the ideal. Life doesn't always allow the ideal, however. If you start your study with the last section and then go through from back to front, you'll still be fine. Do whatever works best for you and your schedule and for your treasured little (or not-so-little) offspring.

introduction

It can happen anywhere. In the car. Watching TV. Reading a good book. At the supper table. In church. You're going about your daily business when one simple thought enters your head, and pain stabs you like a knife. Or you look at your son or your daughter, your heart swells with love for them—their youth and beauty and the wonderful possibilities ahead of them—and without warning, the danger and horrors that could also await them boil up in your gut with heart-stopping anguish.

Worry.

Its effects can be as painful as a physical illness. It takes away your breath, along with your confidence and faith. It crushes your trust in others and in God himself. Yet, unlike many physical illnesses, worry can be controlled, and it can be defeated.

These words are written or said so easily, so glibly. Victory over worry, however, is not always so easily accomplished. Its difficulties and setbacks should not be minimized. But the battle is too important to ignore or to admit defeat.

So what's the answer? Where's the solution?

When you're sleepless at night, worried about kidnappers or rapists or unkind teachers or car accidents or cancer or broken bones or—the list could go on forever—what do you do? Is there a pill? A quick dose of worry suppressant you can take?

Well, *no*.

But there are solutions. And victory can be achieved! The only sure method to defeat worry is to just plain get rid of it. In several short, to-the-point passages, the Bible instructs you to give your worries to God, to pray to him about them, and then to trust him. The result? Freedom from worry! And a peace of mind and spirit you never thought possible.

The six sessions in this study will face head-on the reality of worry in a mother's life—and the only way to conquer it:

♣ **session 1: worry's worthlessness**
What good does it do? Everyone knows it accomplishes

nothing. But one look at your child and thoughts of the terrible things that could happen to him or her pierce your heart. Worry's power can debilitate and make you ineffective as a parent.

❧ session 2: worry's critical consequences
Your children will respond to life's situations as you respond. When their mom is consumed by worry, they'll tend to worry, to approach life with hesitancy — assuming the worst instead of the best. Such concerns snuff out peace and joy and spiritual growth.

❧ session 3: worry or concern?
You worry about things over which you have no control. Legitimate concern involves things over which you do have at least some control. This session will help you distinguish between the two.

❧ session 4: living positively or negatively
Living with negative or positive emotional reactions to your life situation is something that comes naturally. Your genetics and environment incline you to approach life one way or the other. But it's also something you can change. You can use God's Word to approach life with a positive attitude.

❧ session 5: worry-free living
Easier said than done, of course. This session will focus on how to begin to win the battle over a worry-filled lifestyle.

❧ session 6: a weapon against worry
Prayer. It's the only effective weapon against the terrors of uncertainty. This session will reveal the effective ways in which prayer can reduce the power of worry.

You may have trouble believing it at times, but you *can* win the battle over worry in your life. With help from your friends and from God and his Word, you can replace worry with confidence in God. Let's get going!

session 1

worry's worthlessness

For You Alone

Check each situation below that applies to you.
I tend to worry when . . .

- ❏ I'm awake in the dark hours of the night.
- ❏ my daughter goes out on her first date.
- ❏ my child is sick.
- ❏ I remember some of the bad things that happened to me as a child.
- ❏ my husband is late coming home from work.
- ❏ no one answers the phone when I know my kids are home.
- ❏ I read the newspaper.
- ❏ I send my child off to school.
- ❏ I talk to my friends.
- ❏ I answer the phone and no one is there.
- ❏ I watch TV.
- ❏ I think about the future.
- ❏ I plan a trip.
- ❏ I plan to stay home.
- ❏ I'm driving in the car.
- ❏ I'm out for a walk.

- ❏ I'm riding in an airplane.
- ❏ I _____.

How many worry situations did you check? If you checked more than five or six, you just may have a problem with worry.

> When I look back on all these worries, I remember
> the story of the old man who said on his deathbed
> that he had had a lot of trouble in his life,
> most of which had never happened.
>
> WINSTON CHURCHILL

For You and God's Word

Turn for your time in God's Word to Luke 12:25–26. You'll spend more time in this passage in "For You and Others," but for now just look at these two short verses:

> Who of you by worrying can add a single hour to his life?
> Since you cannot do this very little thing,
> why do you worry about the rest?

The New International Version includes a footnote to the word "life," which says, "Or *single cubit to his height.*" In others words, can anyone, by worrying, grow taller? Silly question, isn't it?

- What can you accomplish by *worrying* about your height?
- What can you accomplish by *worrying* about the length of your life? About anyone's life?
- What can you accomplish by *worrying* about your health? About a loved one's health?
- What can you accomplish by *worrying* about your child's safety?
- What can you accomplish by *worrying* about your child's commitment to God?
- What can you accomplish by *worrying* about food or clothes or finances?

By now the answer to all of these questions is probably plain. You accomplish *nothing*. Nada. Zip. Zero. Zilch.

So why bother?

Of course that's easier said than done. More so for some than others. Some people are natural worriers. Others struggle only at certain times or in particular circumstances. No matter whether you're a full-time member of the nail-biting club or an occasional attendee, worry brings you only one place: a dead end.

> *Worry is like a rocking chair: it will give you something to do, but it won't get you anywhere.*
>
> UNKNOWN

Now name three things you're likely to find at that dead end of worry:

What did you come up with? Did you list things like a churning stomach? How about ulcers? Or a lack of faith in God? Or a lack of trust in other people, even those you know to be trustworthy? Did you perhaps think of what your worry does to your family? Children who are fearful? Or a husband who's exasperated?

Okay, so maybe worry does accomplish something. But it's all negative. It adds up to another reason to look at worry as nothing but a huge, solid, unforgiving brick wall. Keep running toward it, and you're bound to get bruised.

For You and Others

Read together Luke 12:22-34. If someone in your group is good at dramatic reading, have her read it aloud, perhaps speaking it as Jesus may have spoken it to his disciples.

> *So I tell you, don't worry about everyday life—whether you have enough food to eat or clothes to wear.* ²³*For life consists of far more than food and clothing.* ²⁴*Look at the ravens. They don't need to plant or harvest or put food in barns because God feeds them. And you are far more valuable to him than any birds!* ²⁵*Can all your worries add a single moment to your life? Of course not!* ²⁶*And if worry can't do little things like that, what's the use of worrying over bigger things?* ²⁷*Look at the lilies and how they grow. They don't work or make their clothing, yet Solomon in all his glory was not dressed as beautifully as they are.* ²⁸*And if God cares so wonderfully for flowers that are here today and gone tomorrow, won't he more surely care for you? You have so little faith!* ²⁹*And don't worry about food—what to eat and drink. Don't worry whether God will provide it for you.* ³⁰*These things dominate the thoughts of most people, but your Father already knows your needs.* ³¹*He will give you all you need from day to day if you make the Kingdom of God your primary concern.* ³²*So don't be afraid, little flock. For it gives your Father great happiness to give you the Kingdom.* ³³*Sell what you have and give to those in need. This will store up treasure for you in heaven! And the purses of heaven have no holes in them. Your treasure will be safe—no thief can steal it and no moth can destroy it.* ³⁴*Wherever your treasure is, there your heart and thoughts will also be.*
>
> LUKE 12:22–34 NLT

1. What does Jesus tell you not to worry about (verse 22)?

2. Share with each other your biggest worries and fears.

3. Do you see Jesus' words in verse 22 as an invitation or a command? Explain.

4. What do you think Jesus means when he says that "life consists of far more than food and clothing" (verse 23)? What are these things?

5. Read verses 24 and 29? Shouldn't people plan and work to get food? Explain your answer.

6. Share with the group the results of your study of verses 24–25 in "For You and God's Word."

7. How does worrying demonstrate a lack of faith (verse 28)?

8. What do verses 30–31 say our perspective, our focus, in life should be? How does this affect worrying and its debilitating results?

9. Jesus lovingly sums up his thoughts in verse 32. What does this verse tell you about Jesus? What does it tell you about your heavenly Father? What response would be appropriate?

10. Does Jesus really want you to sell everything you have and give it away (verse 33)? Explain your answer.

11. What do you think Jesus means when he says that "the purses of heaven have no holes in them" (verse 33)?

12. What may worry be revealing about your level of trust in God?

13. What can you do to increase your trust and reduce your worry?

> *Worry gives a small thing a big shadow.*
>
> SWEDISH PROVERB

For You and God

Read the passage from Luke 12 again. Use it today to pray your thoughts back to God. Confess any worries that cause you to take your eyes off him and his loving desire to care for you and your family. Confess anything that you focus on more than him. Confess anything you treasure more than you treasure him.

When Jesus tells you that worry is worthless, he means it. He knows your human inclination to spend time and effort and emotion worrying about things that will never happen—things you can do nothing about. But he doesn't condemn. He lovingly asks you to trust in him. Talk to him today and ask for a renewed ability and desire to focus your energy and attention on trusting him.

For You and Your Kids

If you're a worrier by nature, you can easily pass on your fears and worries to your children. In order to avoid this pitfall, try these activities with your kids of all ages:

All Ages

Convene a family meeting to talk about worry. Everyone worries at one time or another. Your school-age children will undoubtedly have things to share that they worry about. You have your own worries, and so does your husband. Encourage everyone to openly share their worries. Assign someone in the family to write down each individual worry.

Now take each item and talk about what worrying about it will accomplish. Most of the time the answer will be *nothing.* Take the discussion a step further and talk about a remedy for each worry, what you can do to *avoid* it, and what you can do *instead* of it.

Spend some time as a family praying over your worry list. Ask God to help you understand that instead of worrying you can put your trust in him.

session 2

worry's critical consequences

For You Alone

In your mind, picture the worst thing that could happen to you or your family. How often do you worry that this event—or something similar—will actually happen? How do these thoughts make you feel?

Now try to picture what your stomach looks like when you worry. All in knots, boiling and churning, aching and hurting. Put together some sort of visual that reveals to others what you feel like when you worry. Perhaps it will be a messy and formless picture made with dark crayons or markers. Or a knotted mess of rubber bands or paper clips. Be creative!

For You and God's Word

> *Worry weighs a person down.*
>
> PROVERBS 12:25 NLT

1. When you worry, do you experience this sense of heaviness described by the writer of Proverbs?

2. How else would you describe your feelings when you worry? Why do you think worry does this to you?

> When anxiety [worry] was great within me,
> your consolation brought joy to my soul.
>
> PSALM 94:19

3. What cure for worry is the psalmist talking about here?

4. What exactly does he mean by "consolation"? Where does this consolation come from?

5. How can you apply this verse when you're struggling with worry?

God's Word is exceedingly practical. Worry does often feel like a weight. Freedom from worry brings joy and relief. Psalm 94:19 offers a clear place you can go when worry overwhelms you, and then it gives a clear picture of the result. This sense of relief and joy usually arrives when you realize what you were worrying about never even happened after all. Your daughter arrives home safely. Whew. Your son's injury isn't life-threatening. Ahhh. Your husband's job is secure. Yes!

How would you like to experience this relief and joy *before* you know the outcome? You can! God will give you a sense of peace and trust in him to replace your worry—a "consolation" that gives rise to joyful living.

For You and Others

Start out your session by sharing your creative works from "For You Alone." How creative were you? As a group read Jesus' story of the farmer who sows seeds (Luke 8:1–15).

1. One verse in this passage speaks directly to an extreme result of worry. Which verse is it? Read this verse again out loud.

2. What other things does Luke say are as dangerous as worry (verse 14)? What do all of these have in common?

3. What does this verse say will happen to one who allows worry to rule? Why is this dangerous?

As a group read Jesus' words regarding the signs that will accompany the end of the age (Luke 21:25-36).

4. This passage also has one verse that speaks directly to an extreme result of worry. Which verse is it? Read it aloud with the whole group.

5. What other things does Luke say are as dangerous as worry (verse 34)?

6. What does this verse say will happen to those weighed down by these things? What does this mean?

7. Why do you think worry causes such dire and dangerous results?

8. What choice is better than worry (verse 36)?

9. How does worry affect one's relationship with God?

10. How will worry affect the future? How will faith in God affect the future? Which is the better choice?

Look again at your visuals from "For You Alone." According to Scripture, allowing worry to gain control in your life can have a more dangerous result than the upset stomach that often goes along with it. Commit to your small group members to pray that each of them will be able to replace worry with faith in God.

For You and God

When the worries of life drag you down, use the words of Psalm 94:19 to frame a prayer to God. First, admit to him that worry and anxiety are closer companions than you'd like them to be. Then ask him to send his own consolation—his comfort and protection—to replace your worry and to fill you with joy instead of discomfort. Finally, thank God for his help, for his love, and for his willingness to replace your fears with his own presence.

For You and Your Kids

Instead of introducing worry into your kids lives, introduce a trust and confidence in God and his ability to take care of them. Each time a fearful or difficult situation comes up, repeat the fact that they can always trust God to help them. If you think it would help them, create some sort of visual as a reminder.

All Ages

Read Psalm 18:2 with your children. The last part of this verse would be a great truth for everyone in your family to memorize together. Encourage your children (and yourself!) to remember it whenever they are worried about something or afraid. By remembering this verse and the God it proclaims, your children's worries can be turned into trust and their fears into the strong confidence that God is with them and will never forsake them:

> *My God is my rock, in whom I find protection.*
>
> PSALM 18:2b NLT

As an extra reminder, give each family member a small, smooth stone to carry in a pocket or backpack or purse. Every time they feel afraid or are worried, they can reach for the stone and remember that God is their *rock*.

session 3

worry or concern?

For You Alone

What are you worrying about? Or is it a legitimate concern? It can be hard to distinguish between the two. Take a quick test and see how you do. Alongside each statement, put a "W" for a worry and a "C" for something that is a legitimate concern:

_____ My child could get hurt climbing trees.

_____ A criminal could kidnap my child.

_____ That teacher is too hard on my child.

_____ Walking alone is dangerous.

_____ Riding the bus is dangerous.

_____ My child's room is too close to the gas furnace.

_____ My baby could fall and get hurt.

_____ My child could get hurt playing football/basketball/soccer/whatever.

_____ Someone could hurt my child.

_____ My child could get cancer.

_____ My child should never run with a stick in his or her hand.

_____ Dirty hands cause disease.

_____ Children with runny noses are not welcome to play with my children.

_____ Most movies are bad for my children.

_____ My children may only read certain types of books.

_____ Influences at school are mostly negative and need to be avoided.

_____ My baby may fall behind others if I don't encourage his or her development.

_____ _____.

The truth of the matter is, you could put either a "W" or a "C" (or both) next to each statement.

You worry about things over which you have no control. Worry inhibits action. Legitimate concern involves things over which you have at least some measure of control. Concern stimulates action. However, legitimate concerns can become worries if you hang on to them after you've exerted whatever control is possible. For example: Your daughter must regularly drive distances late at night. So you teach her the principles of safe driving at night and what to do in case of trouble, and you provide a cell phone. That's a response to a legitimate concern. However, if you still sit up, wide-awake, wondering how she is, that's worry. Another example: Your son wants to play a sport. Almost any sport can cause injury to him. So you make sure that he has the best equipment and that he has learned the principles of safety for that sport. That's a response to a legitimate concern. However, if you sit in the stands biting your fingernails and toenails, convinced that in the next minute or two he'll get hurt, that's worry.

For You and God's Word

> *Commit to the LORD whatever you do,*
> *and your plans will succeed.*
>
> PROVERBS 16:3

The Hebrew word translated "commit" here has a literal meaning of "roll," as in rolling your troubles and worries on to the Lord. He can handle them much better than you ever could!

1. What worries or concerns do you have that you could (or even should) roll on to the Lord? How do you go about doing it?

2. What plans could you make to ease at least some of your worries or concerns?

3. Is this verse a promise that *all* your plans will *always* succeed? Explain.

> Cast your cares on the LORD
> and he will sustain you.
>
> PSALM 55:22

4. Is this verse a promise that nothing bad will ever happen to you or your children? Explain. What *does* this verse promise you? What effect does this promise have on your worries and concerns?

For You and Others

Begin your meeting with a discussion of the difference between legitimate concerns and worries. Is there a definite line between the two, or is the distinction fuzzy? You'll probably discover a wide range of opinions on the subject. Follow up your discussion with these two questions:

1. What does having a legitimate concern accomplish?

2. What does worrying accomplish?

As a group look at several verses from Proverbs 14.

> *The wise woman builds her house,*
> *but with her own hands the foolish one*
> *tears hers down.*
>
> PROVERBS 14:1

3. What wise things can you be doing for your "house"—your family—to help lessen any worries you may have?

4. Have you ever done something to your family that in retrospect was foolish or at least not helpful? What was it and what were the results?

5. Do your failures cause you to worry? What can you do to address this issue?

> *The wise look ahead to see what is coming,*
> *but fools deceive themselves.*
>
> PROVERBS 14:8 NLT

6. What are some specific ways in which looking ahead is a wise thing to do?

7. How can looking ahead be foolish? How can it cause you to worry?

> *Only simpletons believe everything they are told! The prudent carefully consider their steps.*
>
> Proverbs 14:15 NLT

Well, here's a pretty definite definition of who's a simpleton and who's a prudent person. You *don't* need to answer the obvious question—which are you? But *do* discuss these questions:

8. Simpletons are easily duped, believing everything—including things that are really lies. How are lies related to worries?

9. How would you define "prudent"?

10. How would a prudent person handle worries and concerns?

11. Read verse 18 for more about a person who is prudent. What crown does the prudent person wear?

12. How does this knowledge relate to the careful planning of verse 15?

13. What could such knowledge and planning do to your concerns? How could they affect your worries?

> *[She] who fears the LORD has a secure fortress,*
> *and for [her] children it will be a refuge.*
>
> PROVERBS 14:26

14. What can a mother rely on to replace her fears and worries for her children? How would you actually *do* this?

15. How can the refuge you find in God give your children a sense of security?

> *When calamity comes, the wicked are brought down,*
> *but even in death the righteous have a refuge.*
>
> PROVERBS 14:32

16. What does this verse say about calamity?

17. What happens to the wicked when calamity comes? What happens to the righteous?

Here's the reality: Your fears and worries may come true. That's the terror, of course. But even in the ultimate calamity of death, you have a refuge — a place of protection and security — in God. In this world of sin and trouble, nothing is for sure. Nothing except God, that is. So even if the worst happens, you can depend on this: God is still there. So what's the point in worrying?

For You and God

Meditate today on the words of the prophet Habakkuk in Habakkuk 3:16-19. Even when life was at its darkest — and there was plenty for him to worry about! — he declared his trust and *joy* in God. Even when enemies were conquering, crops were failing, the worst was happening — even then he found a reason to praise God. What amazing confidence in God's ability to go with him through life's worst nightmare!

Spend a little time putting these words of Habakkuk into your own words, inserting contemporary problems and fears for those he faced. You can then pray these words to gain confidence in God and to build your trust in him when the fears and worries of life overwhelm you. Ask God to fill you with himself, replacing your worries with his comforting presence.

For You and Your Kids

All Ages

If you or any of your kids are natural worriers, post this verse in a prominent place in your house — on the refrigerator or a cabinet by the kitchen table or wherever you'll see it often:

> When I am afraid,
>   I will trust in you.
>   PSALM 56:3

David wrote these words when his enemies were holding him captive. He had *plenty* to worry about, plenty to fear. His very life was in danger. But he chose instead to trust in God. Talk with your children about the dead end of worry and the blessing of choosing to trust in God when fear strikes.

session 4

living positively or negatively

For You Alone

Check your most natural response to the following life situations to gauge whether you approach life more negatively or positively:

There's an ax hanging over my head.
- ❏ Ahhhhh!!! It's going to fall right on me!
- ❏ That ax isn't going anywhere.

My son just stepped on the bus for his first day of school.
- ❏ There are so many bad, bad people out there.
- ❏ School can be a wonderful experience for him.

My car broke down during rush hour.
- ❏ I'm sure to get hit from behind!
- ❏ Certainly someone will stop and help me.

The phone rings in the middle of the night.
- ❏ Someone died.
- ❏ It's got to be a wrong number.

My mom has cancer.
- ❏ I'm sure she'll die soon.
- ❏ The treatments should make it go into remission.

Personality, upbringing, and past experiences can color our reactions to life situations. Sometimes those who respond negatively to life situations feel as though they're just being realists. They know the bad things that can happen. They've experienced them! But does that mean they're *going* to happen? Of course not. Let's look at what God's Word has to say about these two very different approaches to life.

For You and God's Word

Paul wrote to the believers in the church in Thessalonica, urging them to keep a positive perspective—even when times were tough. Read 1 Thessalonians 5:16-18.

1. How would you define "joy"?

2. When does Paul say you should be joyful (verse 16)?

3. Is it truly possible to be joyful always? Why or why not?

4. When does Paul say you should pray (verse 17)? How can you carry out this mandate?

5. Do you think this continual joy and continual prayer are related? How?

6. When does Paul say you should be thankful (verse 18)? Does this mean you should be thankful for bad things that happen to you? Explain your answer.

7. Why would this sort of joyful, prayerful, thankful attitude be God's will for you (verse 18)?

8. How could this sort of attitude affect your worries and fears?

For You and Others

As a group read aloud what Paul said in Philippians 4:4-8 about living positively, and then together answer these questions:

1. What does Paul say to do "always" (verse 4)? Why do you think he repeats himself?

2. Verse 5 gives one reason for joy; what is it?

3. How can God's presence give you joy, even when you're going through rough times?

4. What things does Paul say it's okay to be anxious about (verse 6)?

5. In this same verse, Paul gives a potent antidote to worry and anxiety. What is it?

6. Share experiences about times God helped you overcome your anxieties. What did you do? What was the end result?

7. What will be the result of following Paul's instruction (verse 7)?

8. How does the peace of God make itself evident in a believer's life?

9. When a mother experiences this sort of peace, what effect does it have on her children?

10. How does this peace "guard" your heart and mind (verse 7)? Guard against what?

11. In verse 8, Paul gets down to the nitty-gritty details of how to live life positively instead of negatively. What eight types of things does Paul tell you to think about? Behind each of these, write one example of something you could focus your mind on.

12. What does focusing your mind on such things do to worry?

For You and God

Reread 1 Thessalonians 5:17 and Philippians 4:6. Spend some time examining your heart and life for things that tilt you toward negative thinking. Be honest with yourself, whether it's something you fear for your children, your husband, your marriage, yourself, whatever. Now bring it to God in constant and consistent prayer. Whenever you start to become stressed-out about it, talk to God about it instead of yourself. Experience for yourself what continual prayer can do for your approach to life.

For You and Your Kids

Many kids complain more than their moms would like: "The food at school is terrible. My teacher isn't nice. My homework is too hard. Church activities aren't fun. This TV show is boring. My clothes are way out of style." When your kids are walking Grumble Boulevard, try to head them off at the pass and direct them instead to Cheerful Street.

Preschool–Elementary

Make a book together with your children that helps them in knowing how to respond to different situations. First, have your kids draw pictures of different life situations, such as those mentioned in "For You Alone"—adapted to your kids' particular ages, of course. Next, use two paper plates, one for a large happy face and one for a large sad face. Talk about each situation and ask your children to describe a happy way to think about each and a sad way to think about each. Encourage them to choose to respond positively to life's situations.

Middle School–High School

Life's difficulties begin to settle on the shoulders of children this age. The realities can make your children anxious and even depressed. When helping them learn to cope with their situation as well as their feelings, a sympathetic yet positive attitude on your part can make all the difference. The expressions on your face—either a smile or a frown—and the way you face your own difficulties with positive or negative responses are often imitated by your kids. Your best method to help them is to gauge your own responses. Talk through positive rather than negative responses, encourage them to choose to be positive, and assure them that you pray for them and their life situations daily.

session 5

worry-free living

For You Alone

What is the biggest fear you have in life? What is the thing you tend to worry about most often or most quickly? What makes your stomach tighten in pain and your mind go off on dark paths? If you have trouble identifying it, review the past four sessions. Does one thing pop up more than others?

Throughout this session on living without worry, you'll be concentrating on gaining control over this primary worry in your life. If you can gain victory over this one, the other, smaller ones will follow.

> *Happy the [woman] who has broken the chains that hurt the mind and has given up worrying, once and for all.*
>
> OVID

For You and God's Word

Begin this time in God's Word with an examination of worry's source. Where does it begin? More to the point, who is the author of worry?

Read 1 Peter 5:8.

1. Who prowls around?

2. How can worry "devour" you?

3. Why would Satan use worry to trip you up?

Read Ephesians 4:27. (While this verse is about the dangers of letting Satan gain control of your anger, the same principle can be applied to worry.)

4. How do you give the devil a "foothold" when you worry? What does that foothold do to worry? To you? To your relationship with God?

Read 2 Corinthians 2:11.

5. How aware are you of Satan's "schemes" in your life when it comes to worry?

6. How would being *aware* of how the devil works make you less likely to worry?

7. How would being *alert* to how the devil works make you less likely to worry?

So who's the instigator of worry? The ol' scheming devil himself. All the more reason to avoid it, wouldn't you agree? Worry is not only a negative force in your life but also something that can become sin—and as such it has serious consequences.

For You and Others

Now that you know that Satan is behind this worrisome inclination to worry, what do you do? As a group begin this time by sharing with each other what you discovered in the "For You and God's Word" section.

Look at what the writer of Ecclesiastes says about life:

> *People who work hard sleep well, whether they eat little or much. But the rich are always worrying and seldom get a good night's sleep.*
>
> ECCLESIASTES 5:12 NLT

1. Why do the rich worry while the poor don't? Discuss why the opposite would seem to be more accurate.

2. How much of what you worry about has to do with what you "own"? Name several of your possessions here.

_____
_____
_____
_____
_____
_____

3. What would happen to your perspective if you recognized and lived as though all these things truly belonged to God, not you?

> [She] seldom reflects on the days of [her] life, because God keeps [her] occupied with gladness of heart.
>
> ECCLESIASTES 5:20

4. Is the writer saying that reflection is bad? Explain your answer.

5. What can constant thinking about the past or the future days of your life produce?

6. According to this verse, what is better than this reflection? Why? How do you go about getting it?

Read Psalm 37:1-9 together, then discuss these questions:

7. Compare the actions of verse 1 with those of verses 3 and 4. How are your daily attitudes and worries affected by these different actions?

8. What does God promise to give you (verse 4)? Does this mean he'll give you anything you ask? Explain.

9. What must happen before God will give you what you ask (verse 5)?

10. If the desire of your heart is freedom from worry, would God be willing to give you this? Explain.

11. What four things do verses 7-8 tell you to do?

12. What does verse 8 say is the result of fretting or worrying? What sort of "evil" is the psalmist talking about here?

13. Summarize the attitude the psalmist urges believers to have in the face of life's challenges.

For You and God

Talk to God about the number one worry you listed in "For You Alone" at the beginning of this session. Be honest with him about how often this worry disturbs you and the devil begins to get a foothold because of it. Ask God to help you be aware of and alert to the devil's work in your life in the arena of worry. Ask him for a clear awareness of his presence at these times so that you can turn from a focus on your worry to a focus on him alone. Place this worry at his feet in your mind and spirit, then leave it there. Tell God that it truly is your heart's desire to delight in him, then ask him to increase this desire and substitute it for worry.

For You and Your Kids

Do you ever wonder how you'll teach your kids the futility of worry if you can't gain freedom over worry yourself? How about enlisting their help, working together to gain freedom?

Preschool

Children this age often have many fears and worries—the dark, monsters, things that go bump in the night! Your best lessons are taught on your knees, physically and figuratively. Together with your fearful children, go to God. Help them to see over and over again that they can trust God to be with them, even when life hurls solid reasons for fear into their pathway.

SESSION FIVE: WORRY-FREE LIVING   **51**

Elementary–High School

Continue to emphasize to your children that freedom from fear and worry can be gained when they move their focus from those fears and worries to God. Acknowledge with them that these lessons are not easily learned, but that they are important. Pray *with* them about their worries, and assure them that you're praying *for* them.

All Ages

As a family gather around your fireplace or an outdoor fire pit in your backyard or at the park or beach. Talk together about all your fears and worries, writing each one down on a separate piece of paper. Take each fear seriously, from the youngest to the oldest, including Mom and Dad. Then talk about how God wants you to focus on him instead of your fears. Take each slip of paper and place it in the fire, solemnly and seriously giving each one to God, committing yourselves to a renewed desire to delight in him and focus on him.

session 6

a weapon against worry

For You Alone

To get you thinking about the weapons you have in your battle with worry, write down one weapon word for each letter of the word *weapon*. To give you an idea, the letter "W" could be "Will" — your will to win over worry. You fill in the rest:

W — Will

E — _____

A — _____

P — _____

O — _____

N — _____

Look through the weapons you wrote down. Which one do you think is the best weapon you have against worry? Put a circle around it. Now move on to discover what God says is the best way to gain victory over worry.

For You and God's Word

> *Do not let your hearts be troubled.
> Trust in God; trust also in me.*
>
> JOHN 14:1

Jesus spoke these words to his disciples shortly before his arrest and death. Without a doubt the disciples knew something was happening. The eager crowds had deserted him; threats from the Jewish leadership were growing louder by the minute; Judas had already left to do his betrayal work. Danger hovered over the disciples like a dark physical presence. Of course they were troubled! Their very lives were in danger! And what does Jesus say? Be strong? Be brave? Be tough?

No.

Jesus speaks a few simple words, summed up like this: "Trust me."

Is his appeal any less true for you today? No matter what dangers you or your family face—whether real or imagined—Jesus asks you to trust him. You can replace all your fears and worries with a prayerful trust in God.

Look again at your "weapon" acrostic. How many of you wrote "Prayer" for "P"? How many of you circled it as the most important weapon against worry?

Check the statement that most accurately reflects how you handle your fears:

- ❏ I pray.
- ❏ I worry.
- ❏ I worry, then I pray.
- ❏ I pray, then I worry.

Probably each statement is true of you at some point. The first statement, though, is the goal. And it's the one Jesus was talking about in John 14:1. You can gain an amazing and fortifying trust in God when you leave your worries and fears with him as you go to him in prayer.

For You and Others

Begin your time together today by sharing the weapons you listed in your acrostic in "For You Alone." Be honest about what you wrote, whether it was only a few or a word for every letter. Then share what you listed as your most important weapon.

> Don't worry about anything; instead, pray about everything. Tell God what you need, and thank him for all he has done. If you do this, you will experience God's peace, which is far more wonderful than the human mind can understand.
>
> PHILIPPIANS 4:6–7 NLT

As a group read these verses aloud and then discuss your answers to these questions:

1. What does Paul say you can worry about?

2. Be that as it may, what things *do* you worry about?

3. What does Paul say you can pray about?

4. What things are easy for you to pray about? What things are more difficult?

5. What does Paul say you should tell God?

6. How easily does worry replace prayer in your life? Put another way, how quickly do you think to pray when worry skitters through your mind and stops there?

7. How should you respond after you've told God what you need? List several practical, lifestyle ways to do this?

8. What does God promise you'll receive if you do all this?

9. Relate an occasion when you truly experienced this peace. What were the details of the event, and how did God's peace come about in your life?

Now turn to Peter's first letter and read his encouraging and comforting words:

> *Give all your worries and cares to God,*
> *for he cares about what happens to you.*
>
> 1 PETER 5:7 NLT

10. What sorts of troubles were the readers of Peter's letter facing?

11. What cares and worries does Peter say you should keep to yourself?

12. How exactly do you give all your worries to God? Is this something that happens naturally? Or does it involve something of your will or determination? Explain your answer.

13. Why is God willing to take on all your worries and cares? What is the result (see Philippians 4:7)?

End this last session together with some honest sharing about your fears and worries. Commit together to turn your troubles over to God and also to pray for each other regarding this matter. Only you know the force of the foothold the dead end of worry exerts in your life. With the help of God and fellow believers—your group members, for example—you *can* gain victory and peace.

For You and God

> *Do not let your hearts be troubled.*
> *Trust in God; trust also in me.*
>
> JOHN 14:1

Use this verse to structure your prayers today. You may be ready to commit to trusting in God instead of being troubled and worried, or perhaps you'll have to confess that this is difficult and ask God to give you the grace and faith you need in order to fully trust him.

Tonight, after your children are sleeping, go into each of their rooms and pray a prayer over them. Tell God that you trust him with their lives and their futures. Commit them fully to God.

Admit freely to God your inclination to worry (he knows all about it anyway). Ask him to give you a renewed focus on him rather than on your troubles and fears, so that you can pray instead of worry, trust instead of fear.

For You and Your Kids

Preschool–Elementary

Make a worry wheel. Name some of the fears you know your kids have. Write each one along the edge of one paper plate. Lay another paper plate over the first, cutting out a small section so that each fear can be individually read. Hook the two plates together in the center with a brass brad so the top one can turn on the bottom one. Below the hole you cut in the top plate, write the words, "PRAY when . . ." Now you can turn your wheel and find the answer to every fear with which you or your child struggles. "Pray when *there's a thunderstorm*." "Pray when *you are alone*." "Pray when *it's dark*." Reassure your kids—and yourself—that whatever your fear may be, God will be with you, willing and able to carry that fear away and give you his peace.

Middle School–High School

As your children grow, the worries and fears may change, but they seldom go away. Help them to learn as early as possible to give these fears over to God instead of hanging on to them. Whether they worry about friendships or what they look like or schoolwork or whatever, assure them that you are praying for them and that God is eager for them to give their worries to him. Share openly that you are committing yourself to handing your fears over to God, and encourage them to do the same.

leader's notes

session 1: worry's worthlessness

Question 1. The everyday things of life.

Question 3. Jesus' words are more a loving invitation than a command. He promises to care for all our needs, so why should we worry? His invitation is to trust in him instead of in ourselves, to allow him to free us from fear and the ill effects of worry.

Question 4. Food and clothing represent the physical needs of life. Life consists of far more than the physical side. We also have emotional, mental, relational, and spiritual elements that require fulfillment.

Question 5. Jesus doesn't necessarily imply that *planning* or *preparation* are wrong. But worrying about our future needs is. It all comes down to a matter of focus or priority. If our primary focus is on God, we'll do our planning with his will and promises in mind. And he'll prove to us over and over again that he can be trusted. If, however, our needs and how they'll get met dominate our lives, our focus is on ourselves and our needs rather than on God, which can lead us to a lifestyle of worry—definitely not a spiritually healthy way of life.

Question 7. When we worry, our eyes are on ourselves and our fears rather than on our faithful God. Instead of having faith that God can handle whatever situation we face, we think about everything we can and can't control about the situation—we worry instead of trusting God.

Question 8. Focusing on God will quickly dispel the worries and fears that can dominate our minds so easily. We leave our problems, troubles, and worries in his hands, which are infinitely more capable than ours.

Question 9. Jesus uses loving words—even a pet name ("little flock")—to tell his followers that there is no reason for worry or fear. If we're putting him first in our lives (making his kingdom our primary concern), he'll respond by carefully and tenderly meeting all our needs. This verse reveals Jesus' affection for his followers, as well as the Father's desire to give us all we need if we just trust him to do it. An appropriate response would be thanksgiving in prayer—but more than that, thanks*living* and a renewed focus on God.

Question 10. More than a command to sell all we have, Jesus invites us to keep our possessions in proper perspective. We own them, and many of them are necessities of life. But none of them can ultimately bring lasting happiness or contentment. When we give away our life sustenance—whether it's bread or money or clothing—we trust God to supply the void we've created as the result of our generosity.

Question 11. Jesus' words paint a beautiful picture of the way we can store up our riches in heaven rather than here. Our wealth there will never grow old and rusty or break down. Since your heavenly purse has no holes, whatever you put into it will be there for you to claim when you experience the joy of eternal life with Jesus.

Question 12. Perhaps that it isn't what it should be? Encourage each participant to privately examine her life for areas, including fears and worries, that draw away from rather than toward God and a fulfilling trust in him.

Question 13. As you commit your mind and heart to a greater trust in God, you can decrease your load of worry. Trust is the most effective way to displace worry. Encourage every member of your group, but especially those who seem to have a greater problem with worry, to take the exercise in "For You and God" seriously. It's a great first step to experiencing freedom from worry.

session 2:
worry's critical consequences

Question 1. Verse 14.

Question 2. The riches and pleasures of life. All of these things focus on self rather than on God.

Question 3. She won't mature spiritually. Someone who is immature in the faith tends to be weak and in danger of falling away from faith in God.

Question 4. Verse 34.

Question 5. Dissipation (wasteful living) and drunkenness.

Question 6. Jesus' return will seem more like a trap than a road to freedom. Because these folks spent their time and energy worrying and dipping into the pleasures of life instead of building their faith and trust in God, Jesus' return will come as a surprise and catch them unprepared.

Question 7. Worry reveals a lack of faith in God. Whenever we replace a focus on God with anything else at all, even with "good" things, we run the risk of growing lukewarm in our relationship with God. Any move away from rather than toward God has dangerous implications, both for this life and for the life to come.

Question 8. Prayer—worry's most potent remedy.

Question 9. Worry reduces our ability to trust God with our families, with ourselves, with all that goes on in our lives.

Question 10. Worry will not affect the future. But our faith in God will enable us to walk each day confident in his love and faithfulness, able to trust him with whatever the future brings.

session 3:
worry or concern?

Question 1. A legitimate concern spurs us to action, to do whatever we can to prevent what we're worrying about from happening.

Question 2. Worrying accomplishes nothing except a churning stomach. Worry tends to inhibit action. You're so busy stoking the flames of worry that there's not much else you can do.

Question 6. Looking ahead in order to exert a certain amount of control over a sequence of events is wise (for example, to plan a family budget, to make an educational plan, and so forth).

Question 7. Looking ahead to wonder and worry about what may happen, about how everything may turn out—this is foolish.

Question 8. Neither are necessarily rooted in reality. Not everything we're told is true; not everything we worry about—in fact, very little of what we worry about—will ever happen.

Question 9. To be prudent is to be wise or cautious or careful.

Question 10. Planning ahead, and then praying and committing the plans to God.

Question 11. A crown of knowledge.

Question 12. The prudent person doesn't just plan ahead but does so wisely and cautiously, which involves studying and recognizing the possibilities so that good plans can be made.

Question 13. Spur us on to action. Knowledge or lack of it, however, usually has little affect on worry. Worry is based on fear rather than knowledge.

Question 14. She can rely on God—something that must be done daily, even moment by moment. Turning our children over to God, replacing our fears with trust in him, doesn't happen just once and then we're good to go. It has to be done over and over again.

Question 15. The security you experience in God's hands will filter down to your kids, giving them the same confidence in God's loving ability to control all the events of life and to be with them, even when the bad things happen.

Question 16. It will surely come.

Question 17. The wicked have no foundation, so they collapse; the righteous find refuge in God.

session 4:
living positively or negatively

Question 1. Rejoice in the Lord. Likely Paul recognized how hard it is for most of us! We need to have it emphasized over and over again.

Question 2. The Lord is near.

Question 3. God's presence can give a sense of peace and well-being even when life is throwing darts of difficulty, stress, and danger. God's presence in our lives gives us the ability not just to get through but to rise above rough times. When we recognize that God is truly with us, our fears and worries can be given to him — the one who is, after all, in control of all things. He knows the future and the past. He knows all the good and the bad possibilities. And he will not leave just because something bad happens. He stays and gives comfort and peace instead of worry.

Question 4. Nothing.

Question 5. Prayer.

Question 7. God will be with us.

Question 8. God's presence in a believer's life even during the hardest times reveals itself in a contentment and peace that permeates her entire life and countenance. Even in tears and sorrow, even in fearful circumstances, God's grace gives her a peace that can't be easily explained — but a real peace nonetheless.

Question 9. A mother's peace flows down to her children. When she faces her worries and fears together with God, she gives her children the tools to fight worry and fear in their own lives.

Question 10. Our hearts and minds are quickly overcome by our own humanity and by the schemes of Satan. Trusting and depending on God puts a guard — a hedge, a fence — around our minds and hearts that the devil cannot penetrate.

Question 11.

- whatever is true
- whatever is noble
- whatever is right
- whatever is pure
- whatever is lovely
- whatever is admirable
- whatever is excellent
- whatever is praiseworthy

Question 12. Leaves no room for worry to gain even the smallest foothold.

session 5:
worry-free living

Question 1. The rich have much more to lose. While the poor may worry about where their next loaf of bread or rent payment is coming from, the rich worry about losing what they have or gaining more and more and more.

Question 2. Anything we think we "own"—children, material possessions, and so forth—is something to worry about. But letting it go—living as though we don't own it (because, of course, we *don't*)—brings a wonderful freedom from worry. If it's God's, let him do the "worrying," and we'll do the trusting.

Question 3. Incredible freedom can be gained from handing over to God for his care and possession all the things we think (or act as though) we own.

Question 4. In the context of this passage, the word *reflect* has a somewhat negative connotation. Too much thinking, too much reflection, according to the writer of Ecclesiastes, only brings us to the dead end of life's meaninglessness. Reflection in and of itself isn't bad. It can be good and even necessary. Reflection, however, that *replaces* enjoyment of life is counterproductive.

Question 5. Stress and worry. The past can't be undone. Considering it and seeking forgiveness for past sins is good. Learning from past mistakes is good. However, continually dwelling on the past (on what we've done wrong or on the good times gone by) only produces an inability to enjoy the present. Constant thinking about the future is futile as well. We have no control over it. It's okay to plan, and it's good to be aware of the pitfalls or rewards of the way our lives are heading. But continually dwelling on the future and its possibilities (both negative and positive) only prevents us from enjoying the present.

Question 6. Reflecting on the joys of *today*—the only time we have any control over. We can't change the past or control the future, but we can influence the present by how we think and act and respond. If we focus on God instead of on ourselves, he'll keep us so occupied with "gladness of heart" (is that a cool thought, or what?) and abundant living (see John 10:10) that yesterday and tomorrow—and all the worries connected with them—lose their power over us.

Question 8. The desires of our hearts. God won't necessarily give us *anything* we ask, but he will give us anything we desire that is influenced by our delight in him. Our delight and focus on him come first.

Question 9. Wholly committing ourselves and our ways to God.

Question 10. You can be sure of it! A desire for freedom from worry is, in effect, a desire to delight God and to delight in him.

Question 11. Be still, wait patiently, don't fret (don't be consumed with worry), and don't be angry all the time.

Question 12. It leads only to evil, danger, harm. Worry leads us down all the wrong paths in life. While trying to prevent something from happening or trying to influence future events, we aim to take control of our lives ourselves instead of giving God full rein. Any turning away from God is "evil" in and of itself, and it produces all sorts of additional "evils": physical sicknesses, mental illnesses, emotional instability, hesitancy about life, our kids turning away from us because we're overprotective, negative attitudes, unpleasant demeanors, anger, frustration—well, it seems that worry can cause just about any evil you can imagine.

Question 13. Don't fret and worry and get angry when we don't see the immediate results for which we're looking. All things happen in God's time, not ours. So a stillness before God and a patient waiting for his perfect timing are in order.

session 6:
a weapon against worry

Question 1. Nothing.

Question 3. Everything.

Question 5. We can tell God what we need.

Question 7. Thank him for hearing your prayer and for answering it. When we pray about something and then pick it back up and worry about it, thankfulness in our lives leaks out. Instead, we pray and then live in confidence that God heard us and will answer. That's a living thankfulness.

Question 8. God promises peace.

Question 10. Living in the dangerous first century of Christianity when persecution and death were often the outcome of living a godly life, these believers faced ridicule and often life-threatening dangers.

Question 11. None! God invites us to give him *all* our worries and cares.

Question 12. In prayer—and in reality. When we talk to God about our cares and worries, we give them to him to deal with. And we don't take them back—or at least we shouldn't. It's exactly where the rubber hits the road for most of us. We can pray and give our troubles to God, then minutes later find ourselves worrying and getting stressed-out about them all over again. Truly handing them over to God takes persistence and a deep trust in God and his loving ability to handle them for us.

Question 13. Because he loves us and desires to give us a peace that is beyond understanding. When everything in life dictates fear and worry, God instead gives a deep-seated peace. What an amazing God we follow!

A Mom's Ordinary Day

Finding Joy in All You Are

Jean E. Syswerda, General Editor
Written by Jean E. Syswerda

A Bible study series addressing the unique needs of moms

The demands of parenting can make you forget who you are besides Mom. Dig into this Bible study and rediscover yourself as a whole person: wife, friend, family member, beautiful person, and, most of all, believer. *Finding Joy in All You Are* will help you discover more about yourself—a unique creation of God—and how to make your life one of purpose, balance, and beauty. Beauty? Yes. You may not have a perfect nose or be the Martha Stewart of your neighborhood, but you're still breathtakingly beautiful to God. He knows you completely, loves you best, and wants to show you who you really are. That's worth celebrating!

The eight Bible studies in this series help women discover God's wisdom on how to be the best mothers, women, and disciples they can be. Each study contains six sessions divided into five flexible portions: For You Alone, For You and God's Word, For You and Others, For You and God, and For You and Your Kids. The last section helps moms share each week's nugget of truth with their children.

Softcover
ISBN: 0-310-24712-8

Pick up a copy at your favorite bookstore!

ZONDERVAN™

GRAND RAPIDS, MICHIGAN 49530 USA
WWW.ZONDERVAN.COM

A Mom's Ordinary Day

Gaining and Being a Friend

Jean E. Syswerda, General Editor
Written by Jean E. Syswerda

A Bible study series addressing the unique needs of moms

No matter where you are in your life as a mom—buried in Cheerios and dirty diapers, or running the family schedule like a well-oiled machine—you need your friends. In many ways, your girlfriends are key kindred spirits, and it's their support and companionship that often gets you through the day. This Bible study explores friendship from a variety of angles, giving examples of several biblical people who were good friends, bosom buddies, soul mates. You'll examine these friendships as well as individual Scripture verses on the ups and downs of having and being a friend. Most of all, you'll learn the value of deepening your companionship with God, the one who created you to give and receive the gift of friendship.

The eight Bible studies in this series help women discover God's wisdom on how to be the best mothers, women, and disciples they can be. Each study contains six sessions divided into five flexible portions: For You Alone, For You and God's Word, For You and Others, For You and God, and For You and Your Kids. The last section helps moms share each week's nugget of truth with their children.

Softcover
ISBN: 0-310-24713-6

Pick up a copy at your favorite bookstore!

ZONDERVAN™

GRAND RAPIDS, MICHIGAN 49530 USA
WWW.ZONDERVAN.COM

A Mom's Ordinary Day

Growing Strong with God

Jean E. Syswerda, General Editor
Written by Jean E. Syswerda

A Bible study series addressing the unique needs of moms

Do you fret about what you're not instead of considering who you are in Christ? Spiritual strength doesn't come from building up your spiritual muscles. It comes from learning to rely on God's strength instead of your own, from recognizing your weaknesses and then leaning on him when you're feeling fragile. Delve into this study and discover your true source of strength. Grow strong in prayer, the Word, fellowship, and worship—and next time you're overwhelmed with whatever life has to throw at you, you'll be astonished at the power and vigor you have in God. As you work your way through this study, you'll meet God, and you'll find spiritual strength for each day.

The eight Bible studies in this series help women discover God's wisdom on how to be the best mothers, women, and disciples they can be. Each study contains six sessions divided into five flexible portions: For You Alone, For You and God's Word, For You and Others, For You and God, and For You and Your Kids. The last section helps moms share each week's nugget of truth with their children.

Softcover
ISBN: 0-310-24714-4

Pick up a copy at your favorite bookstore!

ZONDERVAN™

GRAND RAPIDS, MICHIGAN 49530 USA
WWW.ZONDERVAN.COM

A Mom's Ordinary Day
Mothering without Guilt

Jean E. Syswerda, General Editor
Written by Sharon Hersh

A Bible study series addressing the unique needs of moms

Motherhood and guilt go together like peanut butter and jelly. You feel guilty for not making organic baby food, not keeping up with your scrapbook . . . and don't forget your cluttered house. Does it ever end?

Yes, starting now. This study confronts guilt head-on. It will set your heart free to love, laugh, create, and cuddle, and to play and pray with your children. You'll meet new mentors—biblical women who model the possibilities of guilt-free mothering. As you confront your own guilt, be it over real failures or unrealistic expectations, you will find wonderful opportunities to connect with God. His love banishes all guilt and guides you into freedom in motherhood and all of life.

The eight Bible studies in this series help women discover God's wisdom on how to be the best mothers, women, and disciples they can be. Each study contains six sessions divided into five flexible portions: For You Alone, For You and God's Word, For You and Others, For You and God, and For You and Your Kids. The last section helps moms share each week's nugget of truth with their children.

Softcover
ISBN: 0-310-24715-2

Pick up a copy at your favorite bookstore!

ZONDERVAN™

GRAND RAPIDS, MICHIGAN 49530 USA
WWW.ZONDERVAN.COM

A Mom's Ordinary Day
Making Praise a Priority

Jean E. Syswerda, General Editor
Written by Ruth DeJager

A Bible study series addressing the unique needs of moms

Dishes. Laundry. Nose-wiping and boo-boo kisses. The life of a mom stretches out in predictable pattern of housework and nurturing. This Bible study will inspire you to look up from your daily work and celebrate God's presence, to become more aware of his nearness, power, and availability to you. Let this study challenge you to raise your hands in praise and worship rather than to wring them in boredom and apathy. Start using your voice to sing songs of praise rather than to grumble or complain. When you make praise a priority, you will gain a fresh perspective on the challenges you face, and you will set a new and upbeat tone for your home.

The eight Bible studies in this series help women discover God's wisdom on how to be the best mothers, women, and disciples they can be. Each study contains six sessions divided into five flexible portions: For You Alone, For You and God's Word, For You and Others, For You and God, and For You and Your Kids. The last section helps moms share each week's nugget of truth with their children.

Softcover
ISBN: 0-310-24716-0

Pick up a copy at your favorite bookstore!

ZONDERVAN™

GRAND RAPIDS, MICHIGAN 49530 USA
WWW.ZONDERVAN.COM

A Mom's Ordinary Day

Managing Your Time

Jean E. Syswerda, General Editor
Written by Erin Healy

A Bible study series addressing the unique needs of moms

What? You're too busy? Such is the life of a devoted mom—spending your day doing good things for your family, your community, and the Lord. But is your day so packed you have no time for reflection or for noticing God in the unexpected or for experiencing the joy he has built into your work as a mom, wife, and woman? Delve into this Bible study and discover the vision and purpose God has for you in the order of your days. Find out how to manage your time around that which is truly important, not just that which is good. Learn how God's generous wisdom will help you use all of your time for his glory, while taking care not to waste one precious minute.

The eight Bible studies in this series help women discover God's wisdom on how to be the best mothers, women, and disciples they can be. Each study contains six sessions divided into five flexible portions: For You Alone, For You and God's Word, For You and Others, For You and God, and For You and Your Kids. The last section helps moms share each week's nugget of truth with their children.

Softcover
ISBN: 0-310-24717-9

Pick up a copy at your favorite bookstore!

ZONDERVAN™

GRAND RAPIDS, MICHIGAN 49530 USA
WWW.ZONDERVAN.COM

A Mom's Ordinary Day
Entering God's Presence

Jean E. Syswerda, General Editor
Written by Natalie J. Block

A Bible study series addressing the unique needs of moms

As you work through this study, you will discover that God is always available to you and that you need only mustard-seed faith to move the mountains in your life. Find out how prayer can give you stamina for your daily tasks, wisdom to face your challenges, and renewed passion to walk with God. Learn effective ways to intercede for your husband, your children, your friends, and yourself. The minivan, the shower, the garden . . . anyplace can become a "prayer closet" where you can grow closer to a loving and faithful heavenly Father and find help in your time of need.

The eight Bible studies in this series help women discover God's wisdom on how to be the best mothers, women, and disciples they can be. Each study contains six sessions divided into five flexible portions: For You Alone, For You and God's Word, For You and Others, For You and God, and For You and Your Kids. The last section helps moms share each week's nugget of truth with their children.

Softcover
ISBN: 0-310-24718-7

Pick up a copy at your favorite bookstore!

ZONDERVAN™

GRAND RAPIDS, MICHIGAN 49530 USA
WWW.ZONDERVAN.COM

Women of the Bible

A One-Year Devotional Study of Women in Scripture

Ann Spangler and Jean E. Syswerda

Women of the Bible focuses on fifty-two remarkable women in Scripture—women whose struggles to live with faith and courage are not unlike our own. Far from being cardboard characters, these women encourage us through their failures as well as through their successes. You'll see how God acted in surprising and wonderful ways to draw them—and you—to himself.

This yearlong devotional offers a unique method to help you slow down and savor the story of God's unrelenting love for his people, presenting a fresh perspective that will nourish and strengthen your personal communion with him. Designed for personal prayer and study or for use in small groups, *Women of the Bible* will help you grow in character, wisdom, and obedience as a person after God's own heart.

Hardcover 0-310-22352-0

Pick up a copy at your favorite bookstore!

ZONDERVAN™

GRAND RAPIDS, MICHIGAN 49530 USA

WWW.ZONDERVAN.COM

NIV Women of Faith Study Bible

Experience the liberating grace of God

The Bible to help Christian women experience authentic joy

NIV✠ | NEW INTERNATIONAL VERSION

Most read. Most trusted.

God wants to fill up your days with his wonderful gift of grace and love. Let the *NIV Women of Faith Study Bible* help you remove performance-based barriers between yourself and God. Discover how women in biblical times handled struggles similar to yours; gain confidence in Christ's message of grace and freedom; and celebrate your unique, God-given womanhood. In partnership with Women of Faith, the notes and other helps in this Bible have been written specifically with today's Christian woman in mind, with the main goal of helping you experience the liberating grace of God.

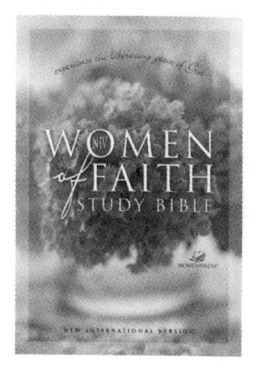

Key features of the *NIV Women of Faith Study Bible* include:

STUDY NOTES. Over 1,700 study notes shed light on the setting, meaning, and application of specific passages or themes. Over two hundred women of the past and present are quoted—from historic writers and poets such as Catherine of Siena and Elizabeth Barrett Browning to Women of Faith speakers/authors Patsy Clairmont, Barbara Johnson, Marilyn Meberg, Luci Swindoll, Sheila Walsh, and Thelma Wells.

CHARACTER SKETCHES. Full-page articles describe the challenges and opportunities of seventy-five women of the Bible. Learn from both the good and the not-so-good responses of these women to their situations and God's activity in their lives.

"ENJOYING GOD" STUDIES. For use individually or in a small group, these fifty-two studies explore key passages that reveal deep meaning and application for you as a woman today.

BOOK INTRODUCTIONS highlight the actions of the women in each book, give pertinent background information, and list all the women who appear in that book.

WOMEN IN JESUS' FAMILY TREE. God's careful selection of women in the Messianic line will inspire hope and purpose for your own life.

NEW INTERNATIONAL VERSION. Most read, most trusted translation.

COMPREHENSIVE STUDY HELPS. A concordance, center-column reference system, and color maps help you get the most out of your Bible study.

The *NIV Women of Faith Study Bible* is a guide you can trust. Filled with insight, it helps you connect with women of the past, present, and future, and it will lead you to new insight as you continue your own journey as a woman of faith.

| Softcover | ISBN 0-310-91884-7 | Black Bonded Leather | ISBN 0-310-92714-5 |
| Hardcover | ISBN 0-310-91883-9 | Violet Bonded Leather | ISBN 0-310-91885-5 |

Pick up a copy at your favorite bookstore!

ZONDERVAN™

GRAND RAPIDS, MICHIGAN 49530 USA

WWW.ZONDERVAN.COM

We want to hear from you. Please send your comments about this book to us in care of zreview@zondervan.com. Thank you.

ZONDERVAN™

GRAND RAPIDS, MICHIGAN 49530 USA

WWW.ZONDERVAN.COM